D0287701

- Barbara -

- 245 Pomponesset Rd.
  Apt

THE
QUEEN

Published by OH!
20 Mortimer Street
London W1T 3JW

Disclaimer:

ISBN 978-1-91161-047-2

Editorial: Stella Caldwell, Victoria Godden
Project manager: Russell Porter
Design: Darren Jordan
Production: Jess Arvidsson

A CIP catalogue for this book is available from the British Library

Printed in Dubai

10 9 8 7 6 5 4 3 2 1

Jacket cover photograph: Theodore Liasi/Alamy Stock Photo

THE
QUEEN

QUOTES TO LIVE BY

CONTENTS

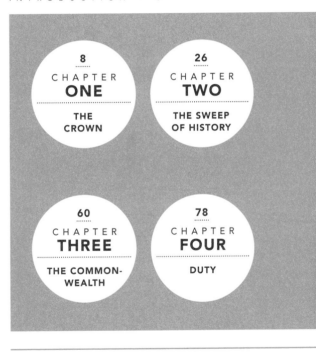

INTRODUCTION

Polls repeatedly show that Queen Elizabeth II is amongst the most admired women in the world. As Britain's longest-serving monarch, she has rarely put a foot wrong in her extraordinary reign. Through wars and upheavals, she has remained a model of composure and calm.

At the time of her coronation in 1953, Winston Churchill was prime minister, Dwight D. Eisenhower president of the United States and Joseph Stalin leader of the Soviet Union. Over seven decades, the queen has criss-crossed the world, engaging with dignitaries and heads of state from India's first prime minister, Jawaharlal Nehru, to US president John F. Kennedy and South African icon Nelson Mandela.

In an address to Parliament in 2002, the queen reflected: "Change is a constant… the way we embrace it defines our future." Her reign has borne witness to the decline of the British Empire and the birth of the Commonwealth of

Nations, Britain's entrance into the European Communities in 1973, the collapse of the Berlin Wall in 1989 and, of course, Brexit in 2020. She reigned through the "Beatlemania" of the 1960s, the election of Britain's first female prime minister, Margaret Thatcher, in 1979, and the birth of the World Wide Web in 1989 (the queen posted on Instagram for the first time in 2019).

Throughout, Prince Philip has remained a constant at the queen's side, while her family has continued to grow and evolve. Like any family, the royals have had to deal with grief, tensions and conflict – and all under the relentless gaze of the media.

Spanning eight decades, the quotes in this book bear witness to the queen's unflappable poise, inspiring dedication to duty and her dry sense of humour, providing a fascinating insight into her public role – and intriguing glimpses of the Elizabeth behind the mask.

CHAPTER
ONE

THE CROWN

66

I declare before you all that my whole life, whether it be long or short, shall be devoted to your service and the service of our great imperial family to which we all belong.

99

Broadcast on her twenty-first birthday, Cape Town, 1947

"

I want to ask you all, whatever your religion may be, to pray for me… to pray that God may give me wisdom and strength to carry out the solemn promises I shall be making, and that I may faithfully serve him and you, all the days of my life.

"

First Christmas broadcast, 1952

66

I have been aware all the time that my peoples, spread far and wide throughout every continent and ocean in the world, were united to support me in the task to which I have now been dedicated with such solemnity.

99

Speech on her coronation day,
2 June 1953

66

I have in sincerity pledged myself to your service, as so many of you are pledged to mine. Throughout all my life and with all my heart I shall strive to be worthy of your trust. **99**

Speech on her coronation day,
2 June 1953

66

I have behind me not only the splendid traditions and the annals of more than a thousand years but the living strength and majesty of the Commonwealth and Empire; of societies old and new; of lands and races different in history and origins but all, by God's will, united in spirit and in aim.

99

Speech on her coronation day,
2 June 1953

“

Therefore I am sure that this, my coronation, is not the symbol of a power and a splendour that are gone but a declaration of our hopes for the future, and for the years I may, by God's grace and mercy, be given to reign and serve you as your queen.

”

Speech on her coronation day,
2 June 1953

"

I loved watching the people and the cars there in the Mall. They all seemed so busy. I used to wonder what they were doing and where they were going and what they thought about outside the palace.

"

Speaking to portrait painter Pietro Annigoni, 1955

Each Christmas, at this time,
my beloved father broadcast a
message to his people in all parts of
the world. Today I am doing this to
you, who are now my people.

First televised Christmas address, 1957

66

I cannot lead you into battle, I do not give you laws or administer justice but I can do something else: I can give you my heart and my devotion to these old islands and to all the peoples of our brotherhood of nations.

99

First televised Christmas address, 1957

66

Within a few feet of where I am standing is the cliff, with its wonderful commanding view over the Thames, which led William the Conqueror to build a castle on this ideal defensive position – a castle which has to this day been the home of kings and queens.

99

Christmas broadcast, 1982

66

Earlier in the year, we marked…
the 300th anniversary of what is
popularly known as the Glorious
Revolution… There are still some
objects here in Buckingham Palace
which bring to life [King] William
and [Queen] Mary as people – and
one which I particularly treasure is
this little patch box that belonged
to the queen and which caries her
monogram entwined with William's
on the lid.

99

Christmas broadcast, 1988

66

Next February will see the fortieth
anniversary of my father's death
and of my accession. Over the years
I have tried to follow my father's
example and to serve you as best I
can… You have given me, in return,
your loyalty and your understanding,
and for that I give you my heartfelt
thanks. I feel the same obligation to
you that I felt in 1952.

99

Christmas broadcast, 1991

"

The link between the Crown and trade and industry is an ancient one. In as much as it serves to foster the very highest standards, it is as relevant today as it ever was.

"

Speech to the Royal Warrant Holder's Association, London, 20 March 2002

The events that I have attended to mark my Diamond Jubilee have been a humbling experience. It has touched me deeply to see so many thousands of families, neighbours and friends celebrating together in such a happy atmosphere. **99**

Broadcast to mark her Diamond Jubilee, 5 June 2012

66

You can't look down to read the speech, you have to take the speech up. Because if you did, your neck would break, it would fall off. So there are some disadvantages to crowns, but otherwise they're quite important things. **99**

Recalling the discomfort of wearing the crown on her coronation day in the BBC programme The Coronation, *January 2018*

"

It's very solid, isn't it?

"

*Examining the solid-gold St Edwards
Crown worn at her coronation, television
interview for the BBC programme
The Coronation, January 2018*

CHAPTER
TWO

THE SWEEP
OF HISTORY

66

Free men everywhere look towards the United States with affection and with hope.

99

To President Harry Truman,
Washington DC, 1 November 1951

"

This new power, which has proved itself to be such a terrifying weapon of destruction, is harnessed for the first time for the common good of our community. A grave responsibility is placed upon all of us to see that man adds as much to his stature by the application of this new power as he has by its discovery.

"

Opening the world's first full-scale nuclear power station at Calder Hall in Cumberland, 17 October 1956

On behalf of the British people, I salute the skill and courage which have brought man to the moon. May this endeavour increase the knowledge and wellbeing of mankind. **"**

Message left on the moon by the crew of Apollo 11, July 1969

"

In the United Kingdom we have our own particular sorrows in Northern Ireland... But there is a light in this tragic situation. The people are steadfastly carrying on their ordinary business... The forces of law and order continue their thankless task with the utmost fortitude in the face of appalling provocation.

"

Christmas broadcast, 1972

It seems to me that Independence Day... should be celebrated as much in Britain as in America. Not in rejoicing in the separation of the American colonies from the British crown but in sincere gratitude to the founding fathers of the great republic for having taught Britain a very valuable lesson...

…We lost the American colonies because we lacked that statesmanship 'to know the right time, and the manner of yielding what is impossible to keep'.

99

Address to the United States marking 200 years since the Declaration of Independence, Philadelphia, 6 July 1976

❝

In 1976, I was reminded of
the good that can flow from
a friendship that is mended…
This year, we went to America
to join in their Bicentennial
celebrations. Who would have
thought 200 years ago that a
descendent of King George III
could have taken part in these
celebrations? Yet that same king
was among the first to recognise
that old scores must be settled…

…The United States was born in bitter conflict with Britain but we didn't remain enemies for long. From our reconciliation came incalculable benefits to mankind and a partnership which, together with many countries of the Commonwealth, was proved in two world wars and ensured that the light of liberty was not extinguished. 99

Christmas broadcast, 1976

66

We face grave problems in the life of our country, but our predecessors, and many alive today, have faced far greater difficulties, both in peace and war, and have overcome them by courage and calm determination. They never lost hope and they never lacked confidence in themselves or in their children. **99**

Christmas broadcast, 1980

66

All this year we seem to have had nothing but bad news, with a constant stream of reports of plane crashes, earthquakes, volcanic eruptions and famine… We hear of riots, wars, acts of terrorism and generally of man's inhumanity to man… Yet there is a lot of good news and some wonderful things are going on in spite of the frightening headlines.

99

Christmas broadcast reflecting on a year that saw an earthquake in Mexico, a volcano in Columbia and famine in Africa, 1985

"

From time to time, we see some inspiring examples of tolerance. Mr Gordon Wilson, whose daughter Marie lost her life in the horrifying explosion at Enniskillen on Remembrance Sunday, impressed the whole world by the depth of his forgiveness.

"

Christmas broadcast reflecting on the terrorist bomb that killed eleven people in Enniskillen in Northern Ireland, 1987

66

We have all been shocked and distressed by a series of major disasters: here in Britain, the worst air crash in our history at Lockerbie and a serious train accident at Clapham; and in Armenia, a terrible earthquake. All three came with great suddenness and destroyed the lives of many people… There are many homes today where the joy of Christmas has been darkened by a cloud of sadness and grief.

99

Christmas broadcast, 1988

Many of you will have heard of the greenhouse effect, and perhaps you've heard too about even more urgent problems caused by the pollution of our rivers and seas and the cutting down of the great forests. These problems don't affect just the countries where they are happening and they make neighbourly co-operation throughout the world a pressing necessity...

…With all your lives before you, I am sure that you take an optimistic view of the future. But it is already too late to prevent all forms of damage to the natural world. Some species of wild plants and animals are, sadly, bound to become extinct. But the great thing to remember is that it is not too late to reduce the damage if we change attitudes and behaviour. **99**

Christmas broadcast, 1989

"

In 1952, when I first broadcast to you at Christmas, the world was a very different place... Only seven years had passed since the end of the most destructive wars in the history of mankind. Even the end of the hostilities did not bring the true peace... as the 'Cold War' sustained an atmosphere of suspicion, anxiety and fear for many years...

…Then, quite suddenly, everything began to change… In 1989, the Berlin Wall came down. Since then the rest of the world has watched, fascinated, as oppressive regimes have crumbled under popular pressure. One by one, these liberated peoples have taken the first hesitant, and sometimes painful, steps towards open and democratic societies.

"

Reflecting on a year that saw Boris Yeltsin win the first public elections to be held in Russia, Christmas broadcast, 1991

"

During a year of wartime commemorations… it has sometimes been tempting to let nostalgia lend a rosy glow to memories of war… Those who suffered the horrors of warfare, in whatever guise, will not have been prey to this temptation. For them, war was not a 'Boys' Own' tale of comradeship and good cheer, but one of hard slog, danger, suffering and exhaustion.

"

Reflecting on the celebrations marking fifty years since the end of the Second World War, Christmas broadcast, 1995

66

I shall never forget the state visit of President Mandela. The most gracious of men has shown us all how to accept the facts of the past without bitterness, how to see new opportunities as more important than old disputes, and how to look forward with courage and optimism.

99

Christmas broadcast, 1996

Think what we would have missed if we had never heard the Beatles or seen Margot Fonteyn dance: never have watched television, used a mobile telephone or surfed the Net (or, to be honest, listened to other people talking about surfing the Net)…

…We would never have heard someone speak from the moon; never have watched England win the World Cup or Red Rum three Grand Nationals. We would never have heard that Everest had been scaled, DNA unravelled, the Channel Tunnel built, hip replacements become commonplace.

99

Reflecting on her fifty-year marriage to Prince Philip, Banqueting House, London, 20 November 1997

History is measured in centuries.
More than ever we are aware of
being a tiny part of the infinite
sweep of time when we move
from one century and one
millennium to another.

Christmas broadcast, 1999

For many people all over the world, the year 2001 seems to have brought them more than their fair share of trials and disasters. But whilst many of these events were of natural origin, it was the human conflicts and the wanton acts of crime and terror against fellow human beings which have so appalled us all.

Reflecting on a year that saw the 9/11 attacks in the United States, Christmas broadcast, 2001

Since 1952, I have witnessed the transformation of the international landscape through which this country must chart its course, the emergence of the Commonwealth, the growth of the European Union, the end of the Cold War and now the dark threat of international terrorism…

…This has been matched by no less rapid developments at home, in the devolved shape of our nation, in the structure of society, in technology and communications, in our work and in the way we live… Change has become a constant; managing it has become an expanding discipline. 99

Speech to mark her Golden Jubilee, Westminster Hall, London, 30 April 2002

66

I take it upon myself to express the immense debt of gratitude we owe to you all. I salute you, and thank you on behalf of our whole nation.

99

Addressing veterans at the sixtieth anniversary D-Day commemoration, Arromanches, 6 June 2004

In remembering the appalling
suffering of war on both sides,
we recognise how precious is the
peace we have built in Europe
since 1945.

*Speech at a German state banquet,
the Zeughaus, Berlin, 2 November 2004*

What were once only hopes for the future have now come to pass; it is almost exactly thirteen years since the overwhelming majority of people in Ireland and Northern Ireland voted in favour of the agreement signed on Good Friday 1998, paving the way for Northern Ireland to become the exciting and inspirational place that it is today.

99

Speech at an Irish state dinner,
Dublin Castle, Dublin, 18 May 2011

I hope people will think very carefully about the future.

Comment to a well-wisher in the days before the Scottish independence referendum, Aberdeenshire, 14 September 2014

Today, as I visit the Science Museum I was interested to discover a letter from the Royal Archives, written in 1843 to my great-great-grandfather Prince Albert.

Her first ever post on the Royal Family's Instagram account, 7 March 2019

66

Visits by American presidents always remind us of the close and longstanding friendship between the United Kingdom and the United States, and I am so glad that we have another opportunity to demonstrate the immense importance that both our countries attach to our relationship. 99

Speech at a state banquet held for President Donald Trump, Buckingham Palace, London, 3 June 2019

"

I hope in the years to come everyone will be able to take pride in how they responded to this challenge. And those who come after us will say that the Britons of this generation were as strong as any…

"

Broadcast to the nation during the coronavirus pandemic, 5 April 2020

66

While we have faced challenges
before, this one is different.
This time we join with all nations
across the globe in a common
endeavour, using the great
advances of science and our
instinctive compassion to heal.
We will succeed – and that
success will belong to every
one of us.

99

Broadcast to the nation during the
coronavirus pandemic, 5 April 2020

CHAPTER
THREE

THE
COMMONWEALTH

"

When it is night and wind and rain beat upon the window, the family is most conscious of the warmth and peacefulness that surround the pleasant fireside. So, our Commonwealth hearth becomes more precious than ever before by the contrast between its homely security and the storm which sometimes seems to be brewing outside, in the darkness of uncertainty and doubt that envelops the whole world.

"

Christmas broadcast, 1954

This year I am thinking of rather a special family – a family of nations – as I recall fascinating journeys to opposite ends of the world. During the course of these visits we met and talked with a great number of people... Yet in all this diversity they had one thing in common: they were all members of the Commonwealth family. **99**

Christmas broadcast, 1970

"

The poet John Donne said: 'No man is an island, entire of itself; every man is a piece of the Continent, a part of the main.' That is the message of the Commonwealth and it is also the Christian message.

"

Christmas broadcast, 1983

66

What a remarkable fifty years
they have been: for the world,
for the Commonwealth and
for Britain.

99

Speech marking the Golden Wedding
anniversary of the queen and Prince Philip,
Banqueting House, London, 20 November 1997

Since I came to the throne in 1952, ten Prime Ministers have served the British people and have come to see me each week at Buckingham Palace. The first, Winston Churchill, had charged with the cavalry at Omdurman. You, Prime Minister [Tony Blair], were born in the year of my coronation…

…You have all had, however, one thing in common. Your advice to me has been invaluable, as has that from your counterparts, past and present, in the other countries of which I am queen. I have listened carefully to it all. I say, most sincerely, that I could not have done my job without it.

99

Speech marking the Golden Wedding anniversary of the queen and Prince Philip, Banqueting House, London, 20 November 1997

Whatever may lie ahead, I declare again here tonight that my admiration, affection and regard for the people of Australia will remain, as it has been over these past fifty years, constant, sure and true. **99**

Speech at Adelaide Festival Hall,
Adelaide, 27 February 2002

66

I retain a deep affection for this great country and for the people who take such pride in saying 'I am Canadian'.

99

Speech in Regina, Saskatchewan, 20 May 2005

66

Atrocities such as these simply reinforce our sense of community, our humanity, and our trust in the rule of law. That is the clear message from us all.

99

Speaking the day after the London terror attacks, Royal London Hospital, 8 July 2005

66

I greatly hope that the Elizabeth Cross will give further meaning to the nation's debt of gratitude to the families and loved ones of those who have died in the service of our country.

99

Broadcast to the armed forces,
1 July 2009

"

This will be the third London Olympiad: my great-grandfather opened the 1908 Games at White City; my father opened the 1948 Games at Wembley Stadium; and later this evening I will take pleasure in declaring open the 2012 London Olympic Games at Stratford, in the east of London.

"

Speech at the Olympic Heads of Government Reception, Buckingham Palace, London, 27 July 2012

66

I feel enormously proud of what
the Commonwealth has achieved,
and all of it within my lifetime. **99**

Speech at the Commonwealth
Heads of Government meeting in Malta,
27 November 2015

66

We expect our homes to be
a place of safety – 'sanctuary'
even – which makes it all the
more shocking when the comfort
they provide is shattered…
Here in London, who can forget
the sheer awfulness of the
Grenfell Tower fire?

99

Christmas broadcast, 2017

66

In April, the Commonwealth Heads
of Government met in London.
My father welcomed just eight
countries to the first such meeting
in 1948. Now the Commonwealth
includes fifty-three countries with
2.4 billion people, a third of the
world's population. Its strength
lies in the bonds of affection it
promotes, and a common desire
to live in a better, more peaceful
world.

99

Christmas broadcast, 2018

"

It is perhaps worth reflecting that at the heart of the word 'Parliament' lies its original meaning: a place to talk. I have no doubt that for most of these last twenty years, this striking chamber has provided exactly that: a place to talk.

"

Speech at the Scottish Parliament marking twenty years of devolution, Holyrood, Edinburgh, 29 June 2019

❝

Commonwealth Day has a special significance this year as we mark the seventieth anniversary of the London Declaration… Today, many millions of people around the world are drawn together because of the collective values shared by the Commonwealth… We are able to look to the future with greater confidence and optimism as a result of the links that we share…

❞

Commonwealth Day message,
8 March 2019

CHAPTER
FOUR

DUTY

I can truthfully say to you all that we children at home are full of cheerfulness and courage. We are trying to do all we can to help our gallant sailors, soldiers and airmen and we are trying too to bear our own share of the danger and sadness of war...

…We know, every one of us, that in the end all will be well, for God will care for us and give us victory and peace. And when peace comes, remember, it will be for us, the children of today, to make the world of tomorrow a better and happier place. 99

*Broadcast from Princess Elizabeth
(aged fourteen) to the children of Britain,
13 October 1940*

Everything I learned was new to me – all the oddities of the insides of a car, all the intricacies of map reading, but I enjoyed it all very much and found it a great experience. **"**

Speaking about her time in the Auxiliary Territorial Service as a junior commander, 1945

We must not be daunted by the anxieties and hardships that the war has left behind for every nation of our Commonwealth. We know that these things are the price we cheerfully undertook to pay for the high honour of standing alone, seven years ago, in defence of the liberty of the world.

Broadcast on her twenty-first birthday, Cape Town, 1947

I simply ache from smiling.
Why are women expected to
beam all the time? It's unfair.
If a man looks solemn, it's
automatically assumed he's
a serious person, not a
miserable one.

*After being criticised for her serious
expression, 1983*

"
Have you come far?

"

*Frequent question when addressing
her garden-party guests, attributed*

"

It's all to do with the training:
you can do a lot if you're
properly trained.

"

Attributed

66

In a way, I didn't have an apprenticeship. My father died much too young and so it was all very sudden... taking on and making the best job you can. It's a question of maturing into something that one's got used to doing, and accepting the fact that it's your fate, because I think continuity is very important. **99**

Interview for the BBC documentary
Elizabeth R, 1992

66

It is a job for life.

99

Commenting on her role as monarch,
interview for the BBC documentary
Elizabeth R, 1992

I do rather begrudge some of the hours I have to do instead of being outdoors.

Commenting on her role as monarch, interview for the BBC documentary Elizabeth R, *1992*

66

One plants one's feet apart like this. Always keep them parallel. Make sure your weight is evenly distributed.

99

On standing still for hours at a time, interview for the BBC documentary Elizabeth R, 1992

66

I can't wear beige because
people won't know who I am.

99

On her dress style, attributed

66

It is my hope that when judged by future generations, our sincerity, our willingness to take a lead, and our determination to do the right thing will stand the test of time.

99

Address to the United Nations,
New York, 6 July 2010

"

I remember my father making me write down what I remembered about his coronation. It was very valuable.

"

Recalling early preparations for her coronation in the BBC programme The Coronation, *January 2018*

CHAPTER
FIVE

THE FIRM

66

In this resolve, I have my husband to support me. He shares all my ideals and all my affection for you. Then, although my experience is so short and my task so new, I have in my parents and grandparents an example which I can follow with certainty and with confidence. **99**

Speech on her coronation day,
2 June 1953

We would like our son and daughter to grow up as normally as possible so that they will be able to serve you and the Commonwealth faithfully and well when they are old enough to do so. We believe the public life is not a fair burden to place on growing children.

Christmas broadcast, 1958

If I am asked what I think about family life after twenty-five years of marriage, I can answer with equal simplicity and conviction, I am for it.

Speech celebrating her Silver Wedding anniversary, Guildhall, London, 1972

66

Don't worry, Betty, I have
one of those at home, too.

99

*To Betty Ford, wife of President
Gerard Ford, after running into her scruffily
dressed son, Jack, during a state visit to the
United States, August 1976*

"

My grandfather, King George V, started the tradition of the Christmas Day broadcasts back in 1932. As he spoke from his study at Sandringham, the 'wireless'… made it possible for millions of people throughout the world to hear the voice of the sovereign for the first time… My father, King George VI, developed [a] theme of optimism and hope, even during the most difficult years of his reign.

"

Christmas broadcast, 1978

66

Last July, we had the joy of seeing our eldest son married amid scenes of great happiness, which made 1981 a very special year for us. The wonderful response the wedding evoked was very moving.

99

Christmas broadcast recalling the wedding of Prince Charles to Lady Diana Spencer, 1981

66

The happy arrival of our fourth grandchild gave great cause for family celebrations. But for parents and grandparents, a birth is also a time for reflection on what the future holds for the baby and how they can best ensure its safety and happiness.

99

Christmas broadcast recalling the birth of Prince Harry, 1984

Like all the best families, we have our share of eccentricities, of impetuous and wayward youngsters and of family disagreements.

Daily Mail, *19 October 1989*

"

My family… has been celebrating my mother's ninetieth birthday, and we have shared with you the joy of some of those celebrations. My youngest grandchild's christening, two days ago, has brought the family together once again. I hope that all of us lucky enough to be able to enjoy such gatherings this Christmas will take time to count our blessings.

"

On a year that saw the queen mother turn ninety and the birth of Princess Eugenie, Christmas broadcast, 1990

1992 is not a year on which I shall look back with undiluted pleasure. In the words of one of my more sympathetic correspondents, it has turned out to be an 'Annus Horribilis'.

Reflecting on a year of family problems, including the separation of Prince Andrew from Sarah, the Duchess of York, and the publication of Andrew Morton's tell-all book Diana: Her True Story, *Guildhall, London, 24 November 1992*

"

I first came here for Christmas as a grandchild. Nowadays, my grandchildren come here for the same family festival. To me, this continuity is a great source of comfort in a world of change, tension and violence.

"

Christmas broadcast from Sandringham, 1992

66

Like many other families, we have lived through some difficult days this year. The prayers, understanding and sympathy given to us by so many of you, in good times and bad, have lent us great support and encouragement. It has touched me deeply that much of this has come from those of you who have troubles of your own.

99

Christmas broadcast, 1992

"

She was an exceptional and gifted human being. In good times and bad, she never lost her capacity to smile and laugh, nor to inspire others with her warmth and kindness. I admired and respected her – for her energy and commitment to others, and especially for her devotion to her two boys.

"

Tribute to Princess Diana, live broadcast to the nation, 5 September 1997

No one who knew Diana will ever forget her. Millions of others who never met her, but felt they knew her, will remember her.

Tribute to Princess Diana, live broadcast to the nation, 5 September 1997

All too often, I fear, Prince Philip has had to listen to me speaking. Frequently we have discussed my intended speech beforehand and, as you will imagine, his views have been expressed in a forthright manner.

Speech marking the Golden Wedding anniversary of the queen and Prince Philip, Banqueting House, London, 20 November 1997

[Prince Philip] is someone who doesn't take easily to compliments but he has, quite simply, been my strength and stay all these years, and I, and his whole family, and this and many other countries, owe him a debt greater than he would ever claim, or we shall ever know.

Speech marking the Golden Wedding anniversary of the queen and Prince Philip, Banqueting House, London, 20 November 1997

❝
...I would say that my mother has much to say to me. Indeed, her vigour and enjoyment of life is a great example of how to close the so-called generation gap. She has an extraordinary capacity to bring happiness into other people's lives. And her own vitality and warmth is returned to her by those whom she meets.

❞

On the queen mother,
Christmas broadcast, 1998

It is hard to believe that a half century has passed since our son Charles was christened, and now, last month, he has celebrated his fiftieth birthday. It was a moment of great happiness and pride on our part in all he has achieved during the last three decades.

Christmas broadcast, 1998

"

As a daughter, a mother and a grandmother, I often find myself seeking advice, or being asked for it, in all three capacities. No age group has a monopoly of wisdom, and indeed I think the young can sometimes be wiser than us.

"

Christmas broadcast, 1998

I cannot forget – and nor can those of us here today who knew her much more personally, as sister, wife, mother or daughter-in-law – the Diana who made such an impact on our lives. **99**

Speech at the opening of the
Diana Memorial Fountain,
Hyde Park, London, 6 July 2004

“

[She] is far too grand for the likes
of us.

”

On Princess Michael of Kent,
The Independent, *4 February 2012*

66

I hope it arrives soon because I'm going on holiday.

On being asked about the imminent birth of Prince William and Kate Middleton's first child, July 2013

99

"

Two hundred years on from the birth of my great-great-grandmother, Queen Victoria, Prince Philip and I have been delighted to welcome our eighth great-grandchild into our family.

"

Reflecting on the birth of Prince Harry and Meghan Markle's son, Archie, Christmas broadcast, 2019

"

My family and I are entirely supportive of Harry and Meghan's desire to create a new life as a young family. Although we would have preferred them to remain full-time working members of the royal family, we respect and understand their wish to live a more independent life as a family while remaining a valued part of my family.

"

Statement from the queen,
13 January 2020

Harry, Meghan and Archie will always be much-loved members of my family. I recognise the challenges they have experienced as a result of intense scrutiny over the last two years and support their wish for a more independent life...

…I want to thank them for all their dedicated work across this country, the Commonwealth and beyond, and am particularly proud of how Meghan has so quickly become one of the family. It is my whole family's hope that today's agreement allows them to start building a happy and peaceful new life.

99

Statement from the queen,
18 January 2020

CHAPTER
SIX

OBSERVATIONS

66

Trafalgar Square, Piccadilly,
Pall Mall, walked simply miles.
Saw parents on balcony at
12.30am – ate, partied,
bed 3am!

99

Diary entry during the
VE Day celebrations, 8 May 1945

66

In the turbulence of this anxious
and active world, many people are
leading uneventful, lonely lives.
To them dreariness, not disaster,
is the enemy. They seldom realise
that on their steadfastness, on
their ability to withstand the
fatigue of dull, repetitive work,
and on their courage in meeting
constant small adversities, depend
in great measure the happiness
and prosperity of the community
as a whole.

99

Christmas broadcast, 1954

66

We praise – and rightly – the heroes whose resource and courage shine so brilliantly in moments of crisis. We forget sometimes that behind the wearers of the Victoria or George Cross there stand ranks of unknown, unnamed men and women, willing and able, if the call came, to render valiant service.

99

Christmas broadcast, 1954

66

[It] seems a ridiculous disease to catch, especially when it isn't even from one's own children! The doctors say that I have chicken pox quite mildly for a grown-up – but it is not much consolation when one is covered in spots!

99

Letter to Prime Minister Edward Heath on contracting chicken pox at the age of forty-five, 28 November 1971

66

All right for Miss [Joan] Collins, but not really for me.

99

On the fashion for shoulder pads, 1980s

We were terrified of being recognised so I pulled my uniform cap well down over my eyes. We walked through the streets, a line of unknown people linking arms and walking down Whitehall, swept along on a tide of happiness and relief.

Recalling her memories of VE Day (8 May 1945) in an interview for Radio 4, 1985

"

Unlike all the other planets in the solar system, Earth shimmers green and blue in the sunlight and looks a very pleasant place to live. **"**

Christmas broadcast, 1989

"

Winston Churchill, my first prime minister, said that 'the further backward you look, the further forward you can see'.

"

Christmas broadcast, 1999

"

Whether we believe in God or not, I think most of us have a sense of the spiritual, that recognition of a deeper meaning and purpose in our lives, and I believe that this sense flourishes despite the pressures of our world.

"

Christmas broadcast, 2000

"
We are a moderate, pragmatic people, more comfortable with practice than theory.

"

Speech to mark her Golden Jubilee, Westminster Hall, London, 30 April 2002

"

Discrimination still exists. Some people feel that their own beliefs are being threatened. Some are unhappy about unfamiliar cultures. They all need to be reassured that there is so much to be gained by reaching out to others; that diversity is indeed a strength and not a threat.

"

Christmas broadcast, 2004

It matters to all of us what kind of country China's people will build, what role they will play in the world of the twenty-first century, and how this will be perceived by others. **99**

State banquet held for President Xi Jinping, Buckingham Palace, London, 8 November 2005

As Groucho Marx once said,
'Anyone can get old – all you have
to do is to live long enough.' **"**

*Speech marking her eightieth birthday,
Mansion House, London, 15 June 2006*

"
The British constitution has always been puzzling and always will be.

Attributed

The Church has a duty to protect the free practice of all faiths in this country… Woven into the fabric of this country, the Church has helped to build a better society – more and more in active co-operation for the common good with those of other faiths.

Speech at Lambeth Palace, London, 15 February 2012

66

At its heart, engineering is about using science to find creative, practical solutions. It is a noble profession.

99

Speech at the Queen Elizabeth Prize for Engineering, Buckingham Palace, London, 25 June 2013

66

Our peace and prosperity can never be taken for granted and must constantly be tended, so that never again do we have cause to build monuments to our fallen youth.

99

Speech to mark the seventieth anniversary of D-Day, Élysée Palace, Paris, 6 June 2014

66

Everything we do, we do for
the young.

99

*Speech to mark the seventieth anniversary
of D-Day, Élysée Palace, Paris, 6 June 2014*

Of course, reconciliation takes different forms. In Scotland after the referendum many felt great disappointment, while others felt great relief; and bridging these differences will take time.

Christmas broadcast, 2014

66
I have to be seen to
be believed.

99

On not disappearing in a crowd,
attributed

CHAPTER
SEVEN

WE ARE
AMUSED

"
They sound like two cats being strangled.

"

*To her lady-in-waiting on hearing
The Everly Brothers perform
"Cathy's Clown", 1960s*

"

New Zealand has long been renowned for its dairy produce, though I should say that I myself prefer my New Zealand eggs for breakfast.

"

On being hit by eggs thrown by protestors in New Zealand, 26 February 1986

These wretched babies don't come until they are ready. **"**

On the late arrival of her grandchild Princess Beatrice, August 1988

66

I do hope you can see
me today.

99

*Referring to the previous day when
her face was obscured by a White House
podium, address to a joint meeting of
Congress, Washington DC, 16 May 1991*

I hope you're not going to be too loud.

To musician Phil Collins shortly before he performed at a concert at the Royal Albert Hall in honour of guest Nelson Mandela, 11 July 1996

“

Oh, dear, I hope it wasn't anyone important.

”

*To International Development Secretary
Clare Short after her phone rang in her
handbag during a meeting of the Privy Council,
The Independent, 2 May 2002*

"

Have you been playing for
a long time?

To guitarist Eric Clapton,
Buckingham Palace, London,
28 February 2005

"

Are you a guitarist too?

To Jimmy Page of Led Zeppelin,
Buckingham Palace, London, 28 February 2005

66

Oh! That was you, was it?

99

On being told by Brian May of rock band Queen that he had played the national anthem at a Golden Jubilee concert held at Buckingham Palace in 2002, Buckingham Palace, London, 28 February 2005

66

They're better behaved
than she is!

99

*On hearing that Princess Michael of Kent
had said the queen's corgis "should be shot",
attributed*

Football's a difficult business and aren't they prima donnas? But it's a wonderful game.

Speaking to Premier League chairman Sir David Richards, Buckingham Palace, London, 23 November 2006

66

I wondered whether I should start this toast by saying, 'When I was here in 1776...'

99

Referring to President Bush's gaffe earlier in the day when he mistakenly told his audience that Queen Elizabeth had helped the US celebrate its bicentennial in 1776 (instead of 1976), formal dinner, Washington DC, 8 May 2007

66

I can almost feel Mrs Blair's knees stiffening when I come in.

99

Speaking of her meetings with Cherie Blair, the wife of former prime minister Tony Blair, the Independent, *4 February 2012*

"

I've been given two bunches this week. Perhaps they want me dead.

"

On hearing that lily of the valley plants were once used as poison, Chelsea Flower Show, 2016

CHAPTER
EIGHT

WISDOM

66

To what greater inspiration
and counsel can we turn than
to the imperishable truth to be
found in this treasure house,
the Bible?

99

Attributed

The upward course of a nation's history is due in the long run to the soundness of heart of its average men and women.

Christmas broadcast, 1954

66

There are long periods when life seems a small, dull round, a petty business with no point. And then suddenly we are caught up in some great event.

99

First live televised speech, Canada, October 1957

66

It has always been easy to hate and destroy. To build and to cherish is much more difficult.

99

Christmas broadcast, 1957

Today we need a special kind of courage. Not the kind needed in battle, but a kind which makes us stand up for everything that we know is right, everything that is true and honest. We need the kind of courage that can withstand the subtle corruption of cynics, so that we can show the world that we are not afraid of the future.

Christmas broadcast, 1957

Even if the presents we give each other at Christmas-time may only be intended to give momentary pleasure, they do also reflect one all-important lesson. Society cannot hope for a just and peaceful civilisation unless each individual feels the need to be concerned about his fellows.

Christmas broadcast, 1966

The struggles against inhuman prejudice, against squalor, ignorance and disease, have always owed a great deal to the determination and tenacity of women.

Christmas broadcast, 1966

"

I believe that Christmas should remind us that the qualities of the human spirit are more important than material gain. Christ taught love and charity and that we should show humanity and compassion at all times and in all situations.

"

Christmas broadcast, 1973

66

If you throw a stone into a pool, the ripples go on spreading outwards. A big stone can cause waves, but even the smallest pebble changes the whole pattern of the water. Our daily actions are like those ripples, each one makes a difference, even the smallest.

99

Christmas broadcast, 1975

66
Even if the problems seem overwhelming, there is always room for optimism. Every problem presents us with the opportunity both to find an answer for ourselves and to help others. 99

Christmas broadcast, 1978

At Christmas we give presents to each other. Let us also stop to think whether we are making enough effort to pass on our experience of life to our children.

Christmas broadcast, 1979

"

Above all, we must retain the child's readiness to forgive, with which we are all born and which it is all too easy to lose as we grow older. Without it, divisions between families, communities and nations remain unbridgeable.

"

Christmas broadcast, 1984

66

There are many serious and threatening problems in this country and in the world but they will never be solved until there is peace in our homes and love in our hearts.

99

Christmas broadcast, 1986

66

There is no point in regretting the passage of time. Growing older is one of the facts of life, and it has its own compensations.

99

Christmas broadcast, 1987

"

There are all sorts of elements to a free society, but I believe that among the most important is the willingness of ordinary men and women to play a part in the life of their community, rather than confining themselves to their own narrow interests.

"

Christmas broadcast, 1991

66
Let us not take ourselves
too seriously. None of us has a
monopoly on wisdom.

99

Christmas broadcast, 1991

If we can look on the bright side, so much the better, but that does not mean we should shield ourselves from the truth, even if it is unwelcome. **99**

Christmas broadcast, 1993

66

In difficult times, it is tempting for all of us, especially those who suffer, to look back and say 'if only'. But to look back in that way is to look down a blind alley. Better to look forward and say 'if only'.

99

Christmas broadcast, 1996

66

When life seems hard, the courageous do not lie down and accept defeat; instead, they are all the more determined to struggle for a better future.

99

Christmas broadcast, 2008

66

I know of no single formula for success. But over the years I have observed that some attributes of leadership are universal and are often about finding ways of encouraging people to combine their efforts, their talents, their insights, their enthusiasm and their inspiration to work together. 99

Address to the United Nations,
New York, 6 July 2010

It has perhaps always been the case that the waging of peace is the hardest form of leadership of all.

Address to the United Nations, New York, 6 July 2010

66

Grief is the price we pay
for love.

99

*Message from the queen at a
remembrance service for the British victims
of 9/11, 20 September 2011*

Sadly, it seems that it is tragedy that often draws out the most and the best from the human spirit.

Christmas broadcast, 2011

With the benefit of historical hindsight we can all see things which we would wish had been done differently or not at all.

Speech at an Irish state dinner,
Dublin Castle, Dublin, 18 May 2011

"

There are other stories written daily across these islands which do not find their voice in solemn pages of history books, or newspaper headlines, but which are at the heart of our shared narrative.

"

Speech at an Irish state dinner,
Dublin Castle, Dublin, 18 May 2011

Although we are capable of great acts of kindness, history teaches us that we sometimes need saving from ourselves – from our recklessness or our greed.

Christmas broadcast, 2011

We all need to get the balance right between action and reflection. With so many distractions, it is easy to forget to pause and take stock. **99**

Christmas broadcast, 2013

66

The true measure of all our
actions is how long the good in
them lasts.

99

Speech at a French state banquet,
6 June 2014

66

It's worth remembering that it is often the small steps, not the giant leaps, that bring about the most lasting change.

Christmas broadcast, 2019

99

66
We should take comfort that while we may have more still to endure, better days will return: we will be with our friends again; we will be with our families again; we will meet again.

99

Broadcast to the nation during the coronavirus pandemic, 5 April 2020

"

Some cultures believe a
long life brings wisdom. I'd like
to think so.

"

Christmas broadcast, 2018